D1070750

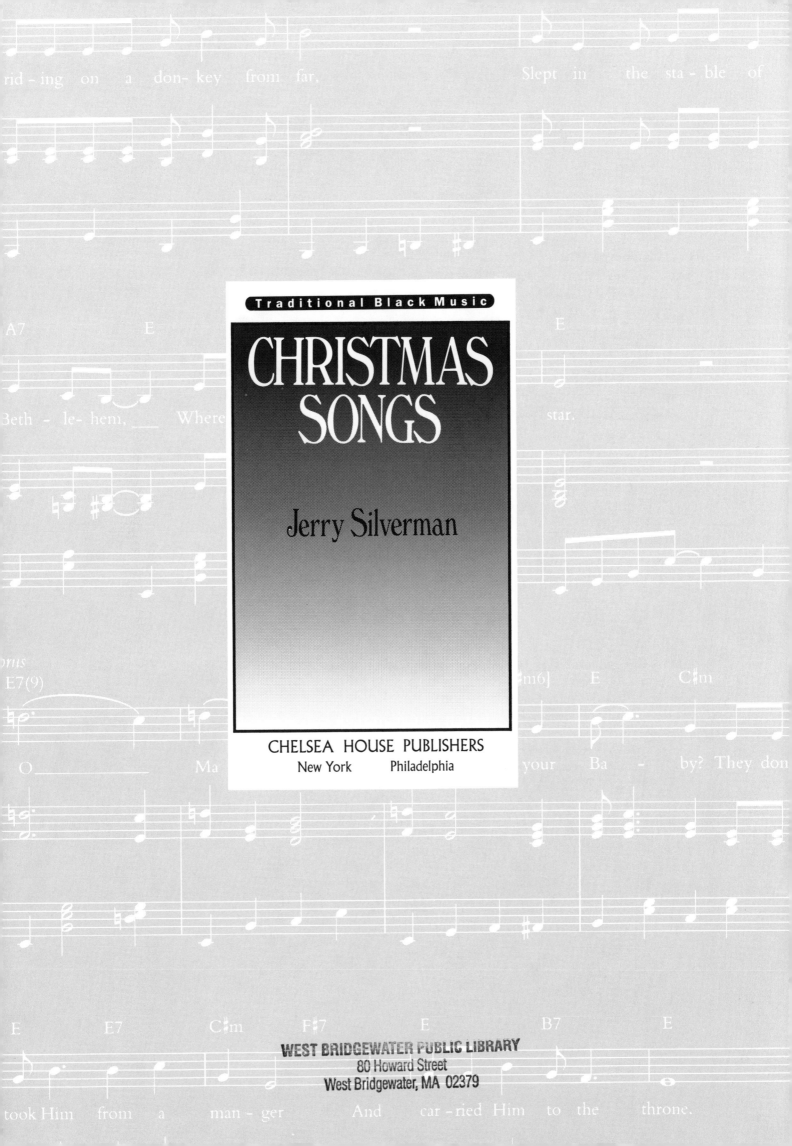

Traditional Black Music

CHRISTMAS SONGS

Jerry Silverman

CHELSEA HOUSE PUBLISHERS

New York   Philadelphia

On the cover Slightly wary but definitely interested, an urban toddler makes his first acquaintance with Santa Claus.

Chelsea House Publishers

Editor-in-Chief   Richard S. Papale
Managing Editor   Karyn Gullen Browne
Copy Chief   Philip Koslow
Picture Editor   Adrian G. Allen
Art Director   Nora Wertz
Manufacturing Director   Gerald Levine
Systems Manager   Lindsey Ottman
Production Coordinator   Marie Claire Cebrián-Ume

Staff for Christmas Songs

Text Editor   Marian W. Taylor
Picture Researcher   Wendy P. Wills
Book Layout   Jesse Cohen, Robert Yaffe

3   5   7   9   8   6   4   2

Library of Congress Cataloging-in-Publication Data

Christmas Songs/[compiled by] Jerry Silverman.
   1 score. — (Traditional black music)
   ISBN 0-7910-1832-6   0-7910-1848-2 (pbk.)
   Christmas music—Juvenile. 2. Afro-Americans—Music. 3. Carols,
English—United States. I. Silverman, Jerry. II. Series.
M1629.3.C5C56 1993   92-756358
                                                        CIP   M

CONTENTS

Author's Preface

The birth of any child is a joyous occasion, the promise of life fulfilled. The birth of a child believed to be humanity's savior is more than an occasion of joy; it is a triumph, a celebration of faith and hope. For black Americans, who first embraced Christianity as slaves, news of a savior's birth delivered a unique message, one with a powerful double meaning.

The Christmas songs of black America reflect that duality. On one hand, they tell of wonder and love for the Infant Jesus, and they urge the faithful to come to Mary's side and to spread the good news of the Redeemer's birth.

On the other hand, these songs also relate to the harsh realities of black life. All believers view the Nativity from their own vantage points: a people in slavery will naturally think of a savior as one who will set them free. White Christians could sing of "peace on earth and goodwill toward men," but their black brothers and sisters had somewhat different priorities: to them, a savior was a practical necessity as well as a spiritual one.

A careful reading of the texts of many black spirituals, Christmas songs in particular, will provide countless examples of the coded language of slaves—phrases with double meanings that would be acceptable to white ears but that would convey a different message to blacks.

Such phrases as "follow the star," "born to set people free," and "steal away" have two parallel sets of meanings: the traditional religious and the down-to-earth secular. They refer to freedom of the soul and to freedom of the individual. When black people sing them today, both interpretations are still valid.

From a historical point of view, these black Christmas songs are crucial to understanding the black experience in America. From a strictly musical point of view, their melodies are sublime, their rhythms infectious. A joy to hear and to sing, they are a precious part of our musical heritage.

Jerry Silverman

The Contribution of Blacks to American Art and Culture

Kenneth B. Clark

Historical and contemporary social inequalities have obscured the major contribution of American blacks to American culture. The historical reality of slavery and the combined racial isolation, segregation, and sustained educational inferiority have had deleterious effects. As related pervasive social problems determine and influence the art that any group can not only experience, but also, ironically, the extent to which they can eventually contribute to the society as a whole, this tenet is even more visible when assessing the contributions made by African Americans.

All aspects of the arts have been pursued by black Americans, but music provides a special insight into the persistent and inescapable social forces to which black Americans have been subjected. One can speculate that in their preslavery patterns of life in Africa, blacks used rhythm, melody, and lyrics to hold on to reality, hope, and the acceptance of life. Later, in America, music helped blacks endure the cruelties of slavery. Spirituals and gospel music provided a medium for both communion and communication. As the black experience in America became more complex, so too did black music, which has grown and ramified, dramatically affecting the development of American music in general. The result is that today, more than ever before, black music provides a powerful lens through which we may view the history of black Americans in a new and revealing way.

Church members celebrate Christmas with a living Nativity scene. In black congregations, such dramatic presentations are often enriched by spirited hymns about Mary and her baby.

In the South's traditional black churches, parishioners do not sit quietly, passively listening to the pastor. They actively participate in the service, responding to their preacher with affirmative shouts and cries. "It Was Poor Little Jesus" is a good musical example of that kind of "leader-response" interaction. In this case, the leader "lines out" the three principal phrases of each verse—essentially, a retelling of the Christmas story—and the congregation affirms each line with an enthusiastic response: "Yes, yes."

IT WAS POOR LITTLE JESUS

Lord, Lord, __ was-n't that a pit-y and a shame? _____

It was poor little Jesus, Yes, yes,
Child of Mary, Yes, yes,
Didn't have no cradle, Yes, yes. *Chorus*

It was poor little Jesus, Yes, yes,
They took him from a manger, Yes, yes,
They took him from his mother, yes, yes. *Chorus*

It was poor little Jesus, Yes, yes,
They bound him with a halter, Yes, yes,
And whipped him up the mountain, Yes, yes. *Chorus*

It was poor little Jesus, Yes, yes,
They nailed him to the cross, Lord, Yes, yes,
They hung him with a robber, Yes, yes. *Chorus*

It was poor little Jesus, Yes, yes,
He's risen from darkness, Yes, yes,
He's ascended into glory, yes, yes. *Chorus*

It was poor little Jesus, Yes, yes,
Born on Friday, Yes, yes,
Born on Christmas, Yes, yes. *Chorus*

City youngsters check out a Christmas diorama: miniature figures that represent the Magi adoring the Christ Child.

"Mary, What You Gonna Name That Pretty Little Baby?" casts the Virgin Mary in the role of a typical expectant mother who is wondering what to call her new child. In the hummed interjections ("Mmm"), she is thinking it over. The song comes to us from singer Peggy Seeger, who learned it from her mother, folklorist Ruth Crawford Seeger.

MARY, WHAT YOU GONNA NAME THAT PRETTY LITTLE BABY?

Mary, what you gonna name
That pretty little Baby?
Mmm — pretty little Baby.
Mmm — laid Him in a manger.
Glory be to the new-born King.

Some call Him one thing,
I think I'll name Him Jesus.
Mmm — pretty little Baby.
Mmm — I think I'll name Him Jesus.
Glory be to the new-born King.

Some call Him one thing,
I think I'll call Him Emmanuel.
Mmm — pretty little Baby.
Mmm — I'll call Him Emmanuel.
Glory be to the new-born King.

Some call Him one thing,
I think I'll call Him Savior.
Mmm — pretty little Baby.
Mmm — I think I'll call Him Savior.
Glory be to the new-born King.

There is complete and personal identification with the Holy Family in "Yonder Comes Sister Mary": The Virgin is "Sister Mary"; her husband is "Brother Joseph." They are seen as members of the singers' congregation, as real and tangible people. Many spirituals use the name *Mary*. One good example is a song that deals with a much earlier biblical event, the Exodus of the "Hebrew children" from Egypt:

> *Oh, Mary, don't you weep, don't you mourn,*
> *Oh, Mary, don't you weep, don't you mourn.*
> *Pharaoh's army got drowned,*
> *Oh, Mary, don't you weep.*

YONDER COMES SISTER MARY

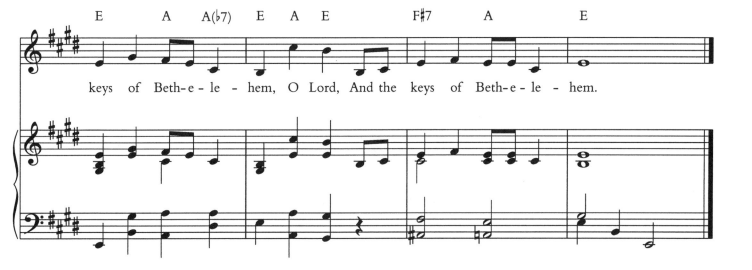

keys of Beth-e-le-hem, O Lord, And the keys of Beth-e-le-hem.

Yonder comes Brother Joseph;
How do you know it is him?
With the palms of vict'ry in his hand,
And the keys of Bethelehem. *Chorus*

Yonder comes Baby Jesus;
How do you know it is Him?
With the palms of vict'ry in His hand,
And the keys of Bethelehem. *Chorus*

A four-year-old Los Angeles girl takes a starring role—that of "Sister Mary"—in her nursery school Christmas pageant.

In the deceptively simple "Bright Morning Stars," Christmas dawn brings forth a complex set of realizations. There is a powerful sense of continuity: as surely as each day—and each generation—follows the last, life will go on. There is also a strong affirmation of eternal life: those no longer here to greet the Savior or to pray have gone, "shouting" with joy, to their heavenly reward.

The song's changing meter (4/4, 5/4, 3/4) reflects the fact that it had no structured accompaniment. The singer was thus free to hold notes "a little longer" and, as the spirit dictated, to pause for emphasis at critical points.

BRIGHT MORNING STARS

Oh, where are our dear fathers,
Oh, where are our dear fathers,
Oh, where are our dear fathers,
Day is a-breaking in my soul.

Some have gone to heaven shouting,
Some have gone to heaven shouting,
Some have gone to heaven shouting,
Day is a-breaking in my soul.

Some are down in the valley praying,
Some are down in the valley praying,
Some are down in the valley praying,
Day is a-breaking in my soul.

Some have gone to greet the Baby,
Some have gone to greet the Baby,
Some have gone to greet the Baby,
Day is a-breaking in my soul.

Christmas morning brings bright smiles (and an array of presents) to three young men and their proud parents.

"Singing in the Land" is one of the "zipper songs" so often found in black folk music: any appropriate word may be substituted ("zipped in") for the first, or key, word of each verse. Another well-known song that follows this pattern is "Kumbaya," in which many of the actions that are also described in "Singing in the Land" are zipped in:

Someone's singing . . . (or shouting, praying, preaching, etc.)
Kumbaya . . . Oh, Lord, kumbaya . . .

SINGING IN THE LAND

Sis - ter, don't you want to go to heav - en? O _____ sis - ter don't you

want to go to heav - en? O _____ sis - ter, don't you

want to go to heav - en? Ba - by of Beth - e - le - hem.

Praying in the land,
Praying in the land,
Praying in the land,
I'm a long ways from home.
Praying in the land,
Praying in the land,
Baby of Bethelehem. *Chorus*

Similarly

Mourning...

Preaching...

Rejoicing...

The railroad is a recurring and powerful image in black American folk song. "The freedom train," "the lonesome train," "the gospel train," and other evocations of the rushing locomotive and its rattling cars abound. It is no accident that John Henry, the great black folk hero who "died with his hammer in his hand," was a railroad worker. "A man," said John Henry to his captain, "ain't nothin' but a man."

Like many spirituals, "Mary Had a Baby" contains a pointed reference to missing a train ("the train done gone"), which may be interpreted as a serious warning to sinners and doubters: "Get on board," or accept Jesus, while there is still time.

MARY HAD A BABY

What did she name Him?
 O, Lord.
What did she name Him?
 O, my Lord.
What did she name Him?
 O, Lord;
The people keep a-coming and the train done gone.

She called Him Jesus,
 O, Lord.
She called Him Jesus,
 O, my Lord,
She called Him Jesus,
 O, Lord;
The people keep a-coming and the train done gone.

Where was He born?
 O, Lord,
Where was He born?
 O, my Lord,
Where was He born?
 O, Lord;
The people keep a-coming and the train done gone.

Where was He born?
 O, Lord,
Where was He born?
 O, my Lord,
Where was He born?
 O, Lord;
The people keep a-coming and the train done gone.

Born in a stable,
 O, Lord,
Born in a stable,
 O, my Lord,
Born in a stable,
 O, Lord;
The people keep a-coming and the train done gone.

Where did they lay Him?
 O, Lord,
Where did they lay Him?
 O, my Lord,
Where did they lay Him?
 O, Lord;
The people keep a-coming and the train done gone.

They laid Him in a manger,
 O, Lord,
They laid Him in a manger,
 O, my Lord,
They laid Him in a manger,
 O, Lord;
The people keep a-coming and the train done gone.

Most black folk songs have a two-beat or a four-beat pulse; three-quarter time is an unusual meter for a traditional black Christmas song. "Jehovah Hallelujah" sounds like a borrowing from an English or Dutch hymn, which is not surprising when we consider that Christianity was brought to the slaves by their masters, most of them Protestants of northern European descent. As James Weldon Johnson (1871–1938), the celebrated black poet, songwriter, and diplomat, once put it, "The Negro took as his basic materials his native African rhythms and the King James Version of the Bible and out of them created the spirituals."

JEHOVAH HALLELUJAH

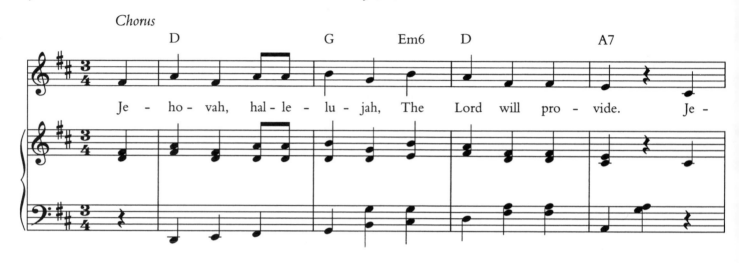

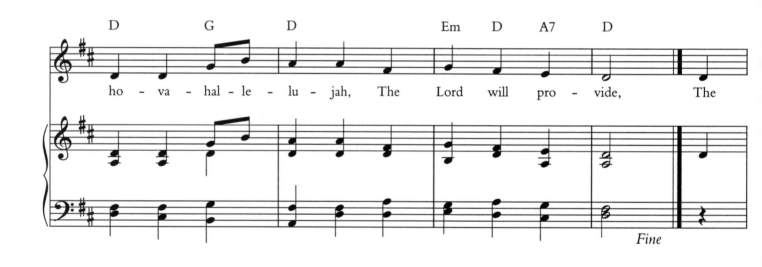

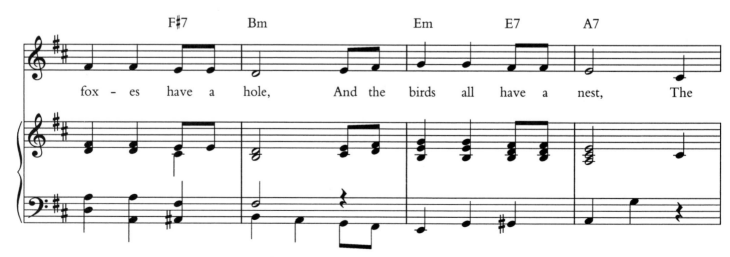

Son of God he ___ dun - no where to take his wea - ry rest.

D.C. al Fine

The animals they came
From far and from near,
To witness the birth
Of the Baby so dear. *Chorus*

The sweet little Babe,
Lying there on the straw;
The greatest of miracles
The world ever saw. *Chorus*

A Baptist dramatic group presents the Bethlehem manger scene: Joseph and the Magi kneel as Mary gazes at her newborn son with awe.

In "Sing-a-Lamb," once again the leader tells the well-known story of the Nativity, and once again the faithful respond, in this case by repeating the song's title: "Sing-a-lamb." As in "Sing Hallelu," no rhymes are needed; anyone can throw out a new line. The melody of the chorus is particularly notable for its unexpected raised fourth note of the scale (G sharp).

SING-A-LAMB

Sing - a- lamb. Bring Ma- ry and the Ba - by, Sing- a- lamb. Bring Ma- ry and the Ba - by, __ Sing- a - lamb.

D.C. al Fine

It's young child Jesus,
    Sing-a-lamb.
It's young child Jesus,
    Sing-a-lamb.
It's young child Jesus,
    Sing-a-lamb.
It's young child Jesus,
    Sing-a-lamb.

He's born in a manger,
    Sing-a-lamb.
He's born in a manger,
    Sing-a-lamb.
He's born in a manger,
    Sing-a-lamb.
He's born in a manger,
    Sing-a-lamb.

"It's Almost Day" concentrates on what, to a child, is the most important part of Christmas: morning and the arrival of Santa Claus. The tradition of keeping a vigil for the Christmas morning star is almost as old as the holy day itself, but Santa Claus is a relatively recent arrival. The red-suited gift giver began as Saint Nicholas, a real-life 4th-century bishop known for his generosity and love of children. Brought to the New World in the 17th century by the Dutch, he became San Nicolaas, Sinter Klaas, and finally Santa Claus, the jolly elf who visits sleeping children on the eve of every Christmas.

References to the morning star have been part of the Christmas service in black churches for generations. In 1927, Library of Congress archivist Robert W. Gordon reported on a Christmas service he attended in a black church in Darien, Georgia: "No matter how many other shouts [religious songs combined with rhythmic dance] were used, [the congregation] would return to ["Look-a Day," a song similar to "It's Almost Day"] again and again throughout the night until finally the watchman reported that the morning star had risen." At this point, the faithful joined in singing:

> *Thought I heard Father Johnny say,*
> *Call the nations great and small,*
> *Look up the road at thy right hand,*
> *The star gives its light!*

IT'S ALMOST DAY

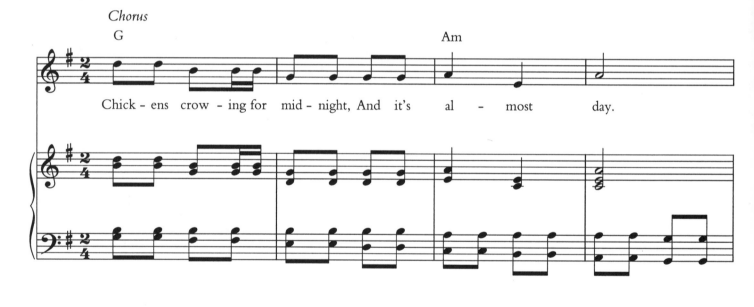

Thought I heard my moth-er say, It's al - most day.

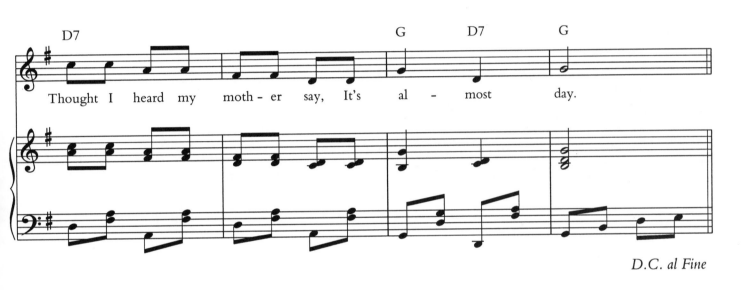

Thought I heard my moth-er say, It's al - most day.

D.C. al Fine

Think I heard my papa say } — *(twice)* *Chorus*
It's almost day.

Christmas is a-coming } — *(twice)* *Chorus*
And it's almost day.

Children are all happy } — *(twice)* *Chorus*
On Christmas Day.

Santa Claus is coming } — *(twice)* *Chorus*
And it's almost day.

This Christmas song bears a striking resemblance, both musically and lyrically, to a later song about a hurricane. "Wasn't That a Mighty Day" tells of the birth of Jesus; "Mighty Day" recounts the tragic events associated with the great hurricane that struck Galveston, Texas, on September 8, 1900:

> *Wasn't that a mighty day,*
> *Wasn't that a mighty day,*
> *Wasn't that a mighty day that morning,*
> *When the storm winds struck the town.*

The Christmas song is undoubtedly much older; as often happens in the folk process, the Galveston song was adapted from it.

WASN'T THAT A MIGHTY DAY

Ly-ing in the sta-ble of Beth- le - hem, _ The beasts did keep-a Him warm.

D.C. al Fine

The shepherds came to wonder,
They came from far and near.
And they saw a-lying there on the straw,
The little Child a-so dear. *Chorus*

Portraying the Wise Men who brought gifts to Baby Jesus, Tanzanian boys take part in a church Christmas pageant.

Traditional black music abounds with code words. When slaves feared they could be overheard by their masters (which was most of the time), they carefully avoided direct reference to forbidden subjects. Escape and freedom, of course, must have been uppermost in many minds, but in their speech and especially in their songs, slaves only hinted obliquely at such things; they used code words that sounded harmless but that would have powerful meaning to singer and listeners alike. In "I Heard-a from Heaven Today," the suggestion of departure ("Hurry on") may certainly be interpreted as a thinly veiled call to escape to freedom in the "other bright world."

I HEARD-A FROM HEAVEN TODAY

D.C. al Fine

The bell is a-ringing in the other bright world,
And I heard-a from heaven today.
The bell is a-ringing in the other bright world,
And I heard-a from heaven today, *Chorus*

The angels a-singing in the heavenly band,
And I heard-a from heaven today.
The angels a-singing in the heavenly band,
And I heard-a from heaven today. *Chorus*

The trumpet sounds in the other bright land,
And I heard-a from heaven today.
The trumpet sounds in the other bright land,
And I heard-a from heaven today. *Chorus*

Mingled with the joy of the holiday season, somewhere there is always the pain of loneliness, separation, or poverty. Folklorist Alan Lomax first heard "Santa Claus Blues," a poignant reminder that not everyone is surrounded by family and friends at this festive time of the year, at the Central State Prison Farm at Sugarland, Texas, in 1941.

SANTA CLAUS BLUES

Good morn-ing blues, blues, how do you do?

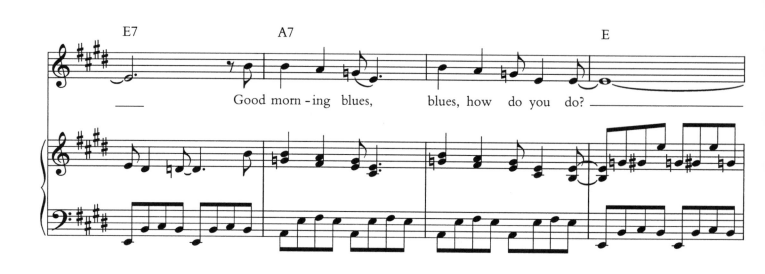

Good morn-ing blues, blues, how do you do?

I feel all right but I've come to wor-ry you.

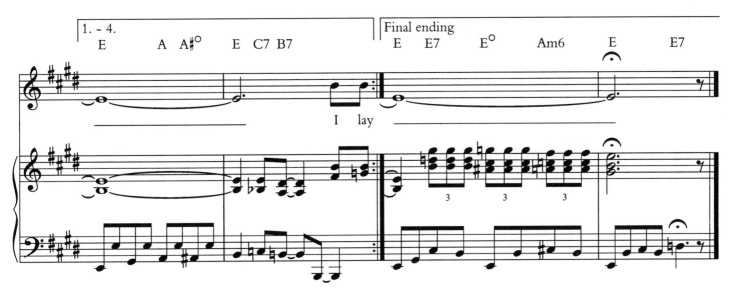

I lay down last night, turning from side to side,
I lay down last night, turning from side to side,
I was not sick, I was just dissatisfied.

I got up this morning, blues walking 'round my bed,
I got up this morning, blues walking 'round my bed,
Went to eat my breakfast, blues was all in my bread.

Well, tomorrow's Christmas and I want to see Santa Claus,
Well, tomorrow's Christmas and I want to see Santa Claus,
If I don't get my baby for Christmas, gonna break all the laws.

Santy Claus, Santy Claus, listen to my plea,
Santy Claus, Santy Claus, listen to my plea,
I don't want nothin' for Christmas but my baby back to me.

The next two songs, both entitled "O, Jerusalem in the Morning," are variations on the same theme, although they are more similar in words than in music. Both songs contain the same homely references to "Mother Mary" and "Father Joseph," familial allusions that serve to humanize the Holy Family and bring them closer to the everyday experiences of the congregation.

O, Jerusalem in the Morning (I)

Moth - er Ma - ry, what is the mat - ter? O, Je - ru - s'lem in the morn - ing,

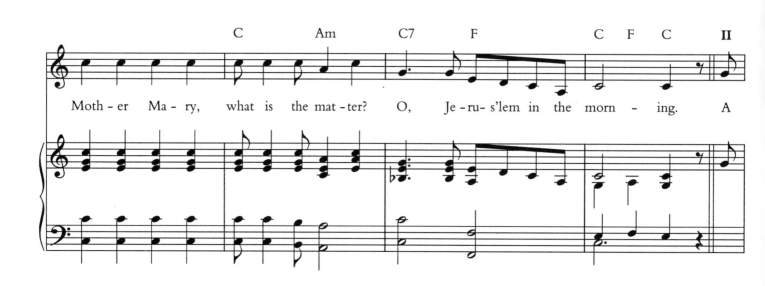

Moth - er Ma - ry, what is the mat - ter? O, Je - ru - s'lem in the morn - ing. A

ba - by born to - day, ___ O, Je - ru - s'lem in the morn - ing.

Born ___ in the man - ger, O, Je- ru- s'lem in the morn - ing.

Sung to Section I:

Father Joseph, what is the matter?
   O, Jerus'lem in the morning.

Sung to Section II:

All wrapped in swaddling clothes,
   O, Jerus'lem in the morning.
Stall was His cradle,
   O, Jerus'lem in the morning.

Born in Bethlehem,
   O, Jerus'lem in the morning.
Born in the manger,
   O, Jerus'lem in the morning.

Jerus'lem, O, Jerus'lem,
   O, Jerus'lem in the morning.
Baby born today,
   O, Jerus'lem in the morning.

O, JERUSALEM IN THE MORNING (II)

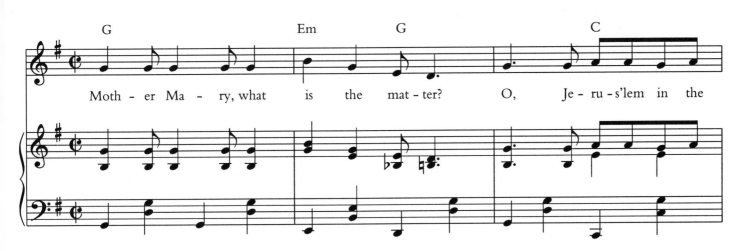

Moth - er Ma - ry, what is the mat - ter? O, Je - ru -s'lem in the

Well, a Baby born today,
  O, Jerusalem in the morning.
Yes, a Baby born today,
  O, Jerusalem in the morning. *Chorus*

Similarly

He was born down in the manger...

They wrapped Him in swaddling clothing...

He was born in Bethlehem...

And the stall it was His cradle...

The first word of "O, Mary, Where Is Your Baby?" is intriguingly ambiguous: Is it *read* in the past tense, reporting what the singer had already discovered in the gospel? Or is it *read* in the imperative mood, urging the listener to study the gospel? Only after we get to the second line ("Read in the gospel and *learn* the news . . .") do we understand it is the imperative *read*: The singer is telling us what to do.

In the song's second verse, the 12-year-old boy who amazes the priest and the tabernacle elders with his wisdom may be the young Jesus, who has just given a perfect recitation of his bar mitzvah lesson.

O, MARY, WHERE IS YOUR BABY?

Read in the gos-pel of Math-a-yew, ___ The gos-pel of Luke ___ and John, Read in the gos-pel and learn the news, ___ How the l'il boy child was born. Read a-bout Ma-ry and Jo- seph, ___ come a-

riding on a donkey from far, Slept in the stable of

Bethlehem, ___ Where the shepherds all seen the star.

Chorus

O_____ Mary, Where is your Baby? They done

took Him from a manger And carried Him to the throne.

Read about the elders and the Hebrew priest,
A-preaching in the tabernacle hall;
Standing in a wonder at the words they heard
From a li'l boy child so small.
"O li'l boy, how old you is?
Tell it if you let it be told.
O li'l boy, how old you is?"
"I ain't but twelve years old."   *Chorus*

All dressed up and on their best behavior, youthful churchgoers attend a Christmas Eve service.

Any time the word *free* or *freedom* appeared in a spiritual, its secular meaning was abundantly clear to all: Freedom now! The key to "The New-Born Baby" is the first line of the second verse: "Born to set the people free." Black spirituals are less concerned with sin than are their white counterparts; they dwell more upon the real troubles of the world, and heaven ("glory") symbolizes an escape, not so much from the temptations of the flesh as from worldly griefs. Black spirituals are filled with an intense yearning for escape from slavery into the heaven of freedom.

THE NEW-BORN BABY

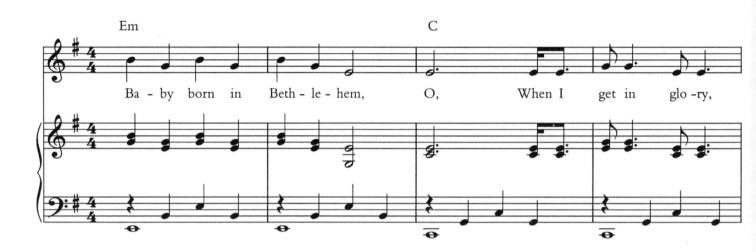

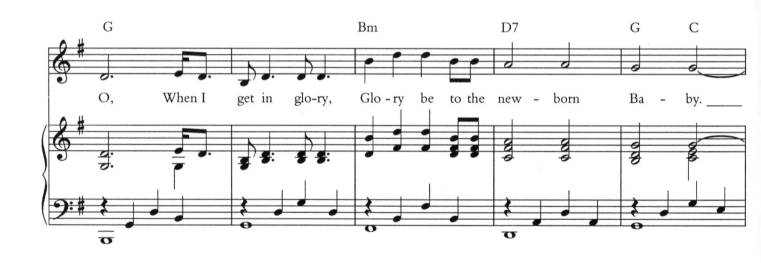

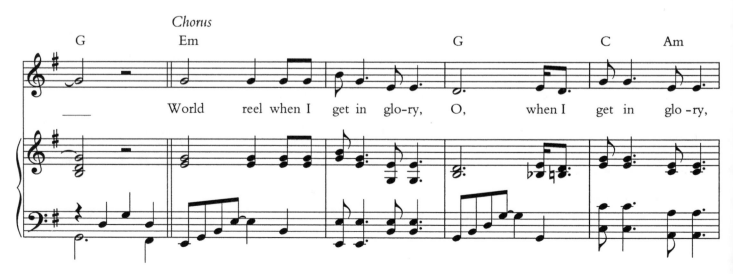

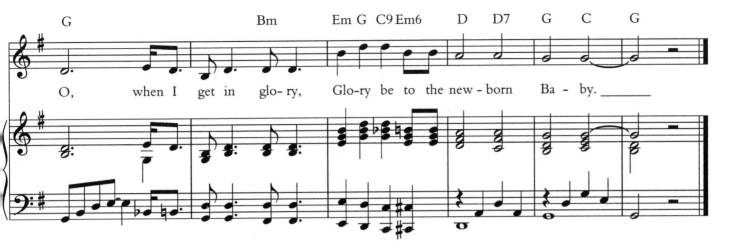

O, when I get in glo-ry, Glo-ry be to the new - born Ba - by. _____

Born to set the people free,
O, when I get in glory,
O, when I get in glory,
Glory be to the new-born Baby. *Chorus*

Born to be the King of Kings,
O, when I get in glory,
O, when I get in glory,
Glory be to the new-born Baby. *Chorus*

German composer George Frederick Handel, who wrote "Joy To the World!" in England in the early 18th century, might have been astonished to hear it sung by a hand-clapping black congregation. (I once heard just such a rendition, and it really swung!) Indicated under the first line of music here is the point at which the off-beat handclaps take place. They should be kept going through the entire song.

JOY TO THE WORLD!

Isaac Watts
(1674 – 1748)

George Frederick Handel
(1685 – 1759)

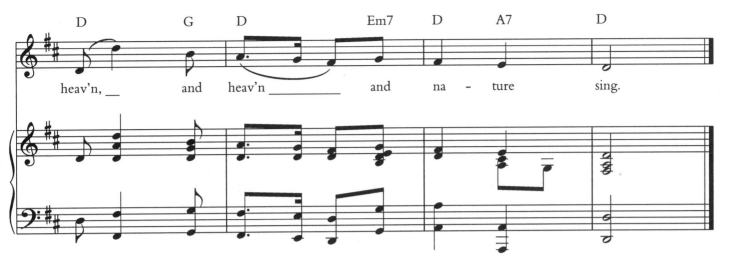

| D | | G | D | | | Em7 | D | A7 | | D |

heav'n, __ and heav'n _____ and na - ture sing.

Joy to the world! the Savior reigns;
Let men their songs employ,
While fields and floods,
Rocks, hills, and plains
Repeat the sounding joy,
Repeat the sounding joy,
Repeat, repeat the sounding joy.

He rules the world with truth and grace,
And makes the nations prove
The glories of
His righteousness,
The wonders of His love,
The wonders of His love,
The wonders, the wonders of His love.

"Santa Claus"—jazz great Lionel Hampton—strikes a joyful chord with young patients at Manhattan's Harlem Hospital.

"Ain't That a Rocking All Night" offers another view of the personalization of Mary as a mother. The image of rocking is strong in black song, appearing in such lines as "Rock-a my soul in the bosom of Abraham" and "One of these nights about twelve o'clock, this old world's gonna reel and rock." In days past, the word *rock* usually referred only to that motion babies find so comforting, but it has taken on a quite different meaning in our own musical times; nevertheless, the "rock" of today's rock music relates directly to the old tradition.

AIN'T THAT A ROCKING ALL NIGHT

Ma - ry had ___ the lit -tle Ba - by, Born in Beth - le - hem.

Ev - 'ry time ___ the Ba - by cry, ___ She rock in a wea - ry land.

Chorus

Ain't that a rock - ing all night, Ain't that a rock - ing all night, ___

Mary bore King Jesus,
Born in Bethlehem,
Every time the Baby cry,
She rock in a weary land. *Chorus*

Mary laid Him in the manger,
Born in Bethlehem,
And every time the Baby cry,
She rock in a weary land. *Chorus*

Writing in the *New York Times* in 1927, folklorist Robert W. Gordon discussed the songs, including "Look-a Day," that he heard in the black churches of rural Georgia. "To have experienced shouting at its best," he noted, "it would have been necessary to attend one of the older churches at Christmas or at New Year's. The service held on Christmas Eve lasted all night long, and interspersed with the shouts were some of the very oldest spirituals. . . . Moreover there were certain special shouts that must traditionally be used on this occasion. The 'watchman,' too, had an added importance, for it was his duty to scan the heavens and announce the first appearance of 'de star.' Shortly after midnight, perhaps when the watchman first went out to seek the star, [the worshipers] were sure to start 'Look-a Day.'"

LOOK-A DAY

O,   o, look -a day,   True   be - liev - er,   O,   o,   look -a day.

Morning starlight,
O, o, look-a day,
Day de comin',
O, o, look-a day.
   Look-a day, look-a day,
   Jump like a member
   Look-a day, look-a day,
   Hop like a member.
True believer,
O, o, look-a day,
True believer,
O, o, look-a day.

Seized by the spirit, southern churchgoers raise their arms and shout with joy during a Christmas Eve service in the 1930s.

The extended chorus of this unusual song takes us on a syncopated journey through the year, climaxing on the last month and its 25th day. The singer is clearly eager to get past the other 11 months, so we can hear the good news about Mary's baby. Alan Lomax, curator of the archives of American folk song at the Library of Congress in Washington, D.C., recorded this song after hearing the great gospel singer Vera Hall Ward sing it in Livingston, Alabama, in 1938.

WHAT MONTH WAS MY JESUS BORN IN?

Tell me what month was my Je-sus born in?
He was born in an ox-stall man-ger,
I'm talking 'bout __ Mar-y's Ba-by,
Last month of the year. __

Tell me what month was my Je-sus born in?
He was born in an ox-stall man-ger,
I'm talking 'bout ___ Mar-y's Ba-by,

Last __ month of the year. Well, you got Jan-u-ar-y,

Feb - ru - ar - y, March, Oh, ___ Lord, __ You got ___

A - pril, May and June, Lord, __ you got Ju - ly, Au - gust, Sep -

tem - ber, Oc - to - ber and ____ No - vem - ber, You got the

twen - ty - fifth day of De - cem - ber; Last __ month __ of the year.

A song such as "O, Mary and the Baby, Sweet Lamb" can continue as long as anyone can come up with an appropriate line. No rhyme is called for; all that is needed is rhythm and sincere feelings. As with many other songs in this collection, the verses given here represent just a small sampling of what might fit comfortably into the lyrics. Some readers may enjoy making up a few verses of their own.

O, Mary and the Baby, Sweet Lamb

It's a holy Baby, sweet Lamb,
It's a holy Baby, sweet Lamb,
It's a holy Baby, sweet Lamb,
O, Mary and the Baby, sweet Lamb. *Chorus*

I love that Baby, sweet Lamb,
I love that Baby, sweet Lamb,
I love that Baby, sweet Lamb,
O, Mary and the Baby, sweet Lamb. *Chorus*

It's a God-sent Baby, sweet Lamb,
It's a God-sent Baby, sweet Lamb,
It's a God-sent Baby, sweet Lamb,
O, Mary and the Baby, sweet Lamb. *Chorus*

Come see the Baby, sweet Lamb,
Come see the Baby, sweet Lamb,
Come see the Baby, sweet Lamb,
O, Mary and the baby, sweet Lamb. *Chorus*

It's a beautiful Baby, sweet Lamb,
It's a beautiful Baby, sweet Lamb,
It's a beautiful Baby, sweet Lamb,
O, Mary and the Baby, sweet Lamb. *Chorus*

It's Mary's Baby, sweet Lamb,
It's Mary's Baby, sweet Lamb,
It's Mary's Baby, sweet Lamb,
O, Mary and the Baby, sweet Lamb. *Chorus*

The distinctive spirituals born in the black American South were the offspring of a marriage between British church music and West African tribal music. Both traditions, which blended with and reinforced each other, relied heavily on the "call-and-response" pattern, well illustrated by this Christmas song, "Sing Hallelu." As the lead singer tells the story of Christ's birth in straightforward and literal terms, the congregation responds with an enthusiastically syncopated "sing hallelu." No rhyming lines are necessary; the repetition of lines within each verse guarantees that everyone present will be able to catch on and sing along. Because anyone could call out lines for all to sing, such a song could—and often did—go on indefinitely.

Sing Hallelu

Mary had a Baby,
　Sing hallelu,
Mary had a Baby,
　Sing hallelu,
Mary had a Baby,
　Sing hallelu,
Mary had a Baby,
　Sing hallelu.

What did she name Him?
　Sing hallelu,
What did she name Him?
　Sing hallelu,
What did she name Him?
　Sing hallelu,
What did she name Him?
　Sing hallelu.

She named Him Jesus,
　Sing hallelu,
She named Him Jesus,
　Sing Hallelu,
She named Him Jesus,
　Sing hallelu,
She named Him Jesus,
　Sing hallelu.

Where was He born?
　Sing hallelu,
Where was He born?
　Sing Hallelu,
Where was He born?
　Sing hallelu,
Where was He born?
　Sing hallelu.

Born in a stable,
　Sing hallelu,
Born in a stable,
　Sing hallelu,
Born in a stable,
　Sing hallelu,
Born in a stable,
　Sing hallelu.

Choir members punctuate a rousing "call-and-response" carol with rhythmic handclaps.

With its add-on cumulative verse structure, this rousing Christmas spiritual, "Children, Go Where I Send Thee!" is reminiscent of an old English carol, "The Twelve Days of Christmas." The exact significance of the rhyming couplets is difficult to pinpoint, but my consultation with a rabbi and a Protestant minister produced a few speculations. The three Hebrew children: Abraham, Isaac, and Jacob; the four who stood at the door: Daniel, Shadrak, Meshak, and Abednego; the five gospel preachers: Matthew, Mark, Luke, and John, the fifth possibly Peter, Paul, or James. The meaning of couplets six, seven, eight, and nine remains mysterious; the tenth, however, is crystal clear.

CHILDREN, GO WHERE I SEND THEE!

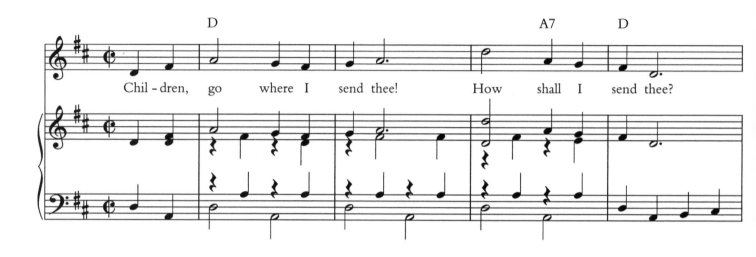

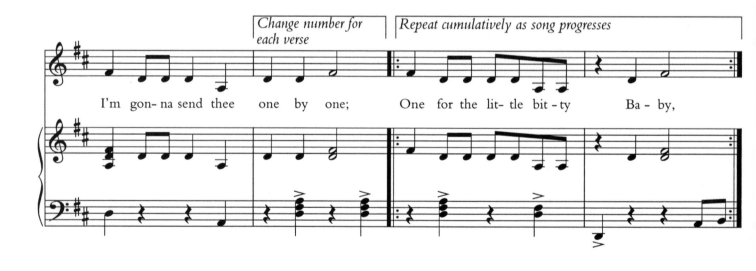

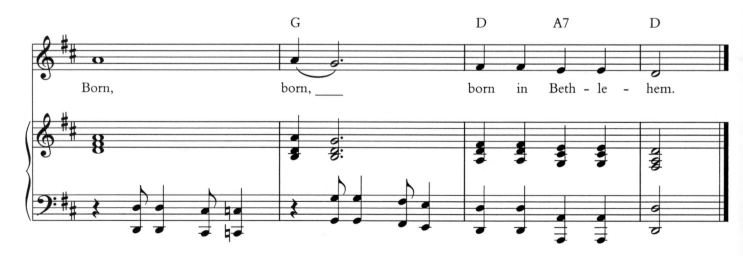

Children, go where I send thee!
How shall I send thee?
I'm gonna send thee two by two;
Two for Paul and Silas,
One for the little bitty Baby,
Born, born, born in Bethlehem.

*Subsequent verses follow the pattern of verses one
and two, adding the numbers three through ten, and
singing back cumulatively to one.*

. . . three by three, Three for the Hebrew children. . .
. . . four by four, Four for the four that stood at the door. . .
. . . five by five, Five for the gospel preachers. . .
. . . six by six, Six for the six that never got fixed. . .
. . . seven by seven, Seven for the seven that never went to heaven. . .
. . . eight by eight, Eight for the eight that stood at the gate. . .
. . . nine by nine, Nine for the nine all dressed so fine. . .
. . . ten by ten, Ten for the Ten Commandments. . .

After the church "watchman" (mentioned in the note on "Look-a Day") had finally announced that day was "broad clear," he would begin to sing "The Angels 'Round the Throne," the closing song of the Christmas service.

THE ANGELS 'ROUND THE THRONE

I want to see my Lord,
I want to see my Lord,
I want to see my Lord,
Crying a-a-a-amen.   *Chorus*

I'm down here on my knees,
I'm down here on my knees,
I'm down here on my knees,
Crying a-a-a-amen.   *Chorus*

Sunday school pupils, each bearing a gift for a less fortunate child, gather around their parish house Christmas tree.

The image of the mountain, its summit close to the heavens, has always exerted a powerful influence on the minds of the faithful: there, one can be alone with one's innermost thoughts. Noah's Ark came to rest upon Mount Ararat; Moses received the Ten Commandments from God on Mount Sinai; to this day, we talk of shouting glad tidings "from the mountaintops." It is no wonder, then, that the "learner"—whom faith has transformed into the messenger in "Go Tell It on the Mountains"—is going to announce the birth of Jesus "on the mountains, over the hills and everywhere."

GO TELL IT ON THE MOUNTAINS

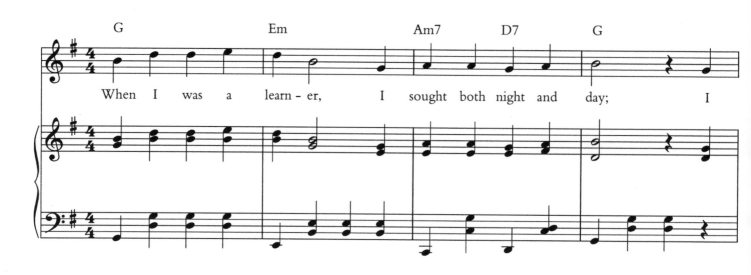

When I was a learn - er, I sought both night and day; I

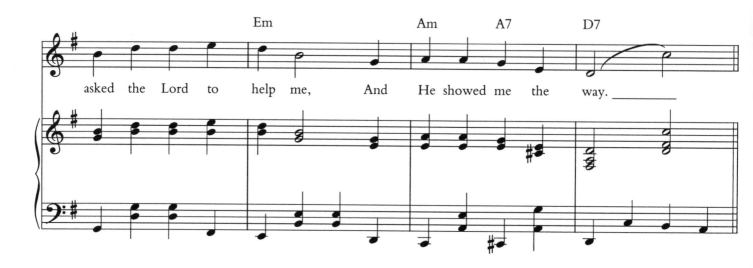

asked the Lord to help me, And He showed me the way.

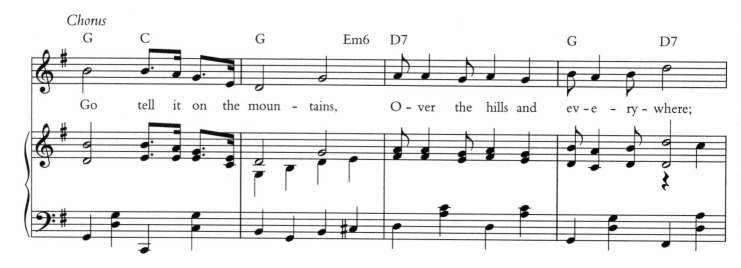

Chorus

Go tell it on the moun - tains, O - ver the hills and ev - e - ry - where;

Go tell it on the moun - tains: Our Je - sus Christ _ is born.

While shepherds kept their watching;
O'er wand 'ring flocks by night;
Behold! From out the Heavens,
There shone a holy light. *Chorus*

And lo, when they had seen it,
They all bowed down and prayed;
Then they traveled on together,
To where the Babe was laid. *Chorus*

The shepherds feared and trembled,
When, lo, above the earth
Rang out the angels' chorus,
That hailed our Savior's birth. *Chorus*

Down in a lowly manger,
Our humble Christ was born,
And God sent us salvation
That blessed Christmas morn. *Chorus*

He made me a watchman
Upon the city wall,
And if I am a Christian,
I am the least of all. *Chorus*

On December 24, 1818, Austrian church organist and composer Franz Xavier Gruber set to music "Silent Night, Holy Night," a Christmas poem by Joseph Mohr. Over the years, in English translation, the song has become a perennial favorite in the United States. When performed by black gospel singers, it invariably undergoes subtle rhythmic changes; some of that feeling is evident in this arrangement.

SILENT NIGHT, HOLY NIGHT

Franz Gruber
(1787 – 1863)

Silent, night, holy night!
Shepherds quake at the sight,
Glories stream from heaven afar,
Heav'nly hosts sing alleluia;
Christ the Savior is born!
Christ the Savior is born!

Silent night, holy night!
Wondrous star, lend thy light!
With the angels let us sing
Alleluia to our King!
Christ the Savior is here,
Jesus the Savior is here!

Many folk songs—especially, of course, those relating to Christmas—tell the same story. The following two spirituals, "Christ Was Born in Bethlehem" and "Jesus Borned in Bethlea," start out in essentially the same manner, using similar words and musical material. "Christ Was Born in Bethlehem," however, goes on to recount much more than the Nativity, whereas "Jesus Borned in Bethlea" is limited to the blessed event itself.

CHRIST WAS BORN IN BETHLEHEM

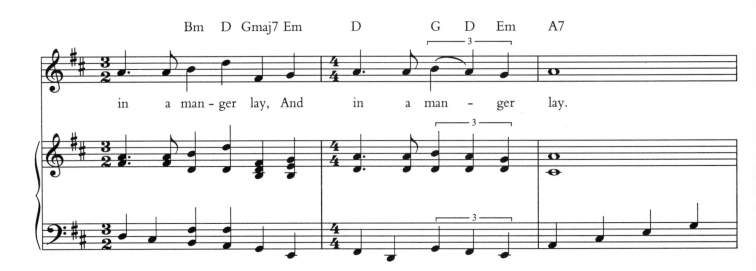

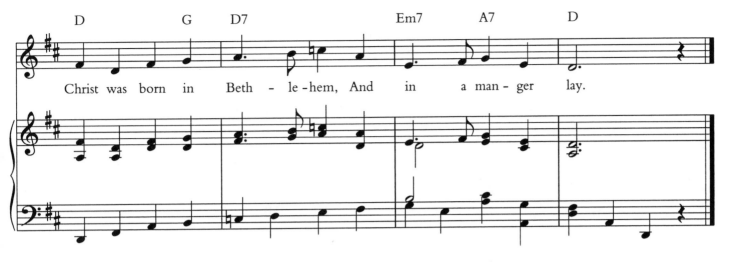

Christ was born in Beth - le -hem, And in a man - ger lay.

Judas, he betrayed Him,
Judas, he betrayed Him,
Judas, he betrayed Him,
And nailed Him to a tree,
And nailed Him to a tree,
And nailed Him to a tree,
Judas, he betrayed Him,
And nailed Him to a tree.

Similarly

Joseph begged His body. . .
And laid it in the tomb. . .

The tomb, it would not hold Him. . .
He burst the bands of death. . .

Down there came an angel. . .
And rolled the stone away. . .

Mary, came a-weeping. . .
Her blessed Lord to see. . .

What's the matter, Mary?. . .
They've stole my Lord away. . .

Go and tell your brethren. . .
He's risen from the dead. . .

JESUS BORNED IN BETHLEA

Je - sus borned in Beth - lea, Je - sus borned in Beth - lea,

Borned on Christmas morning,
Borned on Christmas morning,
Borned on Christmas morning,
And in a manger lay.
   And in a manger lay,
   And in a manger lay.
   Borned on Christmas morning,
   And in a manger lay.

All sing hallelujah,
All sing hallelujah,
All sing hallelujah,
Our Jesus borned today.
   Our Jesus borned today,
   Our Jesus borned today.
   All sing hallelujah,
   Our Jesus borned today.

In slavery days, the call to "rise up and follow" took on a meaning beyond that of the shepherds following the Star of Bethlehem to Christ's manger. The light that guided escaping slaves was the North Star, which could lead them to freedom. "Follow the Drinking Gourd," a celebrated song of the Underground Railroad (the secret network of trails and guides that helped runaway slaves get as far north as Canada), directs its listeners to

> *Follow the drinking gourd,*
> *Follow the drinking gourd,*
> *For the old man is a-waiting for to carry you to freedom,*
> *If you follow the drinking gourd.*

The two outer stars of the bowl of the "drinking gourd"—the constellation also known as the Big Dipper—point to the North Star—and freedom.

RISE UP, SHEPHERD, AND FOLLOW

Beth - le - hem, _____ Rise up shep - herd, and fol - low. _

If you take good heed to the angel's words,
Rise up, shepherd, and follow;
You'll forget your flocks, you'll forget your herds,
Rise up shepherd, and follow. *Chorus*

Following a quartet of altar boys, worshipers and celebrants enter a New York City Episcopal church.

Jerry Silverman is one of America's most prolific authors of music books. He has a B.S. degree in music from the City College of New York and an M.A. in musicology from New York University. He has authored some 100 books dealing with various aspects of guitar, banjo, violin, and fiddle technique, as well as numerous songbooks and arrangements for other instruments. He teaches guitar and music to children and adults and performs in folk-song concerts before audiences of all ages.

Kenneth B. Clark received a Ph.D. in social psychology from Columbia University and is the author of numerous books and articles on race and education. His books include *Prejudice and Your Child, Dark Ghetto,* and *Pathos of Power.* Long noted as an authority on segregation in schools, his work was cited by the U.S. Supreme Court in its decision in the historic *Brown v. Board of Education of Topeka* case in 1954. Dr. Clark, Distinguished Professor of Psychology Emeritus at the City University of New York, is the president of Kenneth B. Clark & Associates, a consulting firm specializing in personnel matters, race relations, and affirmative action programs.